To Sarah, with all best wishes from the authors.

Nigel & Marie-Frances

WILD MUSHROOMS

How to Find, Identify & Cook Them

Nigel & Marie-France Addinall

Illustrated by Irene Bache

Christopher Davies

Published by
Christopher Davies (Publishers) Ltd.,
P.O. Box 403, Sketty,
Swansea, SA2 9BE.

ISBN 0 7154 0661 2

*Typeset by
Dynevor Printing Company,
Llandybïe, Dyfed, Wales*

*Printed by
Jolly & Barber Ltd.,
Rugby, Warwickshire.*

For Raphaël

CONTENTS

ILLUSTRATIONS

WILD MUSHROOMS

FOREWORD

"Is it true," a friend of mine asked me recently, "that you can only eat wild mushrooms for breakfast, or else they make you ill?" This was a variant on the more commonly held theory that you can only find wild mushrooms if you go to look for them at crack of dawn, but both illustrate how little is known about them by most British people, and the suspicion with which they are viewed. The only grain of truth that these beliefs contain is that:

— A mushroom picked and eaten early in the morning will be at its freshest, whereas — like any vegetable or fruit — the longer it is left uneaten the more likely it is to start rotting.

— If you don't go mushrooming early in the morning, somebody else is likely to get to the mushrooms first!

However ludicrous, these beliefs do at least have the merit of recognising that edible mushrooms *can* be found in nature, and that it is not therefore true that anything not bought in a shop will kill you. They refer, however, to one mushroom only, or rather to those members of the *Psalliota* family which are collectively known as the 'field' mushroom; for most British people anything else is a 'toadstool' and will therefore poison you. The British are unfortunately unique in this; every other European country is familiar with at least two or three other kinds of edible mushrooms. What is the reason for this? Is the 'field' mushroom the only one that bears no resemblance to something poisonous? Or could it be that other edible mushrooms just do not grow in Britain, or at least not in sufficient quantities to arouse people's interest? Or that their taste is so insignificant as to make them not worth bothering about? The answer to all three of these is an emphatic 'no', so let us now briefly examine them in turn.

The 'field' mushroom — *Psalliota campestris* and its close cousins *Psalliota arvensis*, *Psalliota silvicola* and *Psalliota silvatica* (see Page 50) — can bear quite a close resemblance, when young, to the deadly poisonous *Amanita phalloïdes* (see Page 14).

On the other hand, such delicious edible mushrooms as *Boletus edulis* (the famous French *cèpe,* see Page 66) or *Cantharellus cibarius* (the equally famous *girolle* or *chanterelle*, see Page 58) cannot be confused with anything dangerous or suspicious at all.

All the wild mushrooms described in this book grow freely in Britain and can be found quite easily by anyone looking in the right places at the right time of year. The 'Identification and Habitat' section devoted to each mushroom in the text will help you to track down your quarry, but do remember that each one requires different soil and climatic conditions and it is not therefore sufficient to find an oak or beech wood to find *cèpes* for example, but you will most certainly not find any without one. When you do find your *cèpe* wood, you can be certain that not only will you find a goodly number of these delicious mushrooms but that they will almost invariably grow in the same places from year to year, and in roughly similar numbers, unless weather conditions have proved unfavourable, which, in Britain, means it has rained too much over the summer and autumn.

It is certain that all mushrooms do not taste the same. If you eat, therefore, a *girolle* (say) expecting it to taste like a 'field' mushroom, you are bound to be disappointed: you must expect it to taste like a *girolle*. In fact the difference in taste between wild mushrooms is such that you can no more compare them than you would compare a potato to a carrot. Just as you would not make chips out of carrots, or make a grated raw potato salad, so you should not prepare all mushrooms in the same way. To make the most of them, therefore, different recipes are needed and these will be found accompanying each mushroom after the 'Identification and Habitat' section.

And so to conclude the Foreword of this book. Its object is to help you find, identify and make delicious meals of those common edible mushrooms which are enjoyed by our European neighbours and which cannot be confused with anything poisonous. And what a total pleasure it all is! A relaxing walk in the woods, the thrill of coming across a 'carpet' of wild mushrooms and gathering them, the delight of preparing them according to your chosen recipe, and the immense pleasure of feasting on them with friends!

I hope I have convinced you and that you will join our select little band devoted to 'mushroom seeking for eating'. If so, this book is for you. If not, and you are still reading on, I can only suppose it is because you have something in common with the personages in the following two little anecdotes. The first involves a coastguard who pulled up beside me in his Land Rover as I was picking 'blewits' (*Tricholoma nudum,* see Page 86) near a beach one day. To reach me he had had to cross some fairly rough terrain and his interest in what I was doing was immediately made apparent: "Do you mean to say you can eat those blue toad-stools?" he asked. After explaining that one could, that they were in fact a delicacy, and — in view of his continued fervent interest — giving him a recipe that you will find in this book, he thanked me profusely, jumped back into his Land Rover, and said: "Well, you won't catch *me* eating one of those things!"

The second anecdote concerns a lady who, contrary to our coastguard, had a very considerable knowledge of fungi. I was newly arrived in the town where I was living and when introduced to her took the opportunity to ask her if she knew of any good local *cèpe* (*Boletus edulis*) woods. She replied that she did and was lucky enough in September/October to take home a dozen or more *cèpes* at a time. "How do you prepare them?" I asked. "Well," she replied, "I cut off the stalks to make sure that they aren't maggoty, then I put the sound caps on white paper until the next day so as to be able to obtain a spore print." "And then?" I asked. "And then," she replied with disarming but devastating simplicity, "I throw them away."

To my mind, this is exactly equivalent to opening a bottle of fine claret, examining it for colour and tannin content, and then pouring it down the kitchen sink! Hopefully, you will not commit such a crime, but will drink your claret with your *cèpes* or other mushrooms, prepared according to one of the recipes contained in this book. However, let us not anticipate, a little clearing of the wood, as it were, needs to be done first.

Amanita phalloides

INTRODUCTION

This book is written for those whose interest lies in eating good wild mushrooms, and not in mycology for its own sake. Two important lessons follow from this: the first is that one must be able to identify with certainty the edible mushrooms, the second is that one must be able to identity with certainty those that are poisonous or that can cause stomach upsets.

Let us deal with the latter initially. Fear of them is so primeval as to be on the level of dread of the wolf, but just as a Pekinese or a Dachsund have practically no physical characteristics in common with the wolf, so our edible mushrooms have next to nothing in common with their poisonous cousins. What, then, do the latter look like?

The first simple observation to be made is that all common fungi belong to one of three main types. Under their caps they have either (a) GILLS, or (b) TUBES, looking much like a sponge, or (c) small SPIKES (see the illustrations below). In fact, there do exist other types, such as the *clavaria* group which are fern or bush like, or the different members of the round puff-ball family, or those, rather like large leathery tongues, that grow on rotting tree trunks or branches, but none of these are of any particular culinary interest, and are not therefore contained in this book, with the exception of the fairly delicious *Pleurotus ostreatus* (or Oyster mushroom, see Page 94) which does grow on dead tree trunks, the absolutely delicious Morel (see Page 42) which looks rather like a sponge on the end of a stalk, and its near cousins the *Helvellas* (see Page 91).

Of the three main groups, the only one that contains deadly poisonous fungi is the one that has gills. It follows that you should never eat a mushroom with gills unless you have had it positively identified by an expert, or you are already totally familiar with the species. Having said this, the only common members of this group which are deadly poisonous are easily identifiable: they are *Amanita phalloïdes* (see Page 14) and its almost indistinguishable cousins *Amanita virosa* and *Amanita verna*.

Of the group that has tubes — sponge-like in appearance — there is only one that is suspected of being capable of causing

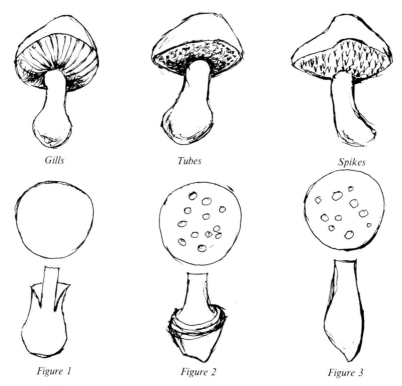

| Gills | Tubes | Spikes |

| Figure 1 | Figure 2 | Figure 3 |

stomach upsets, and even then there are mycologists who consider that its reputation is undeserved: it is *Boletus satanas* (see Page 39).

Of the group that has spikes, there is only one which is generally considered worth eating: *Hydnum repandum* (see Page 87) but there are no poisonous members of this group.

The above indicates that there is little danger of poisoning yourself (and a bare modicum of commonsense should ensure that you do not) but as 'safety first' must be our first rule, the book begins with a detailed description of those fungi which are poisonous or suspect. It continues with a detailed description of those which are edible in, broadly, the order in which they grow during the year — Spring, Summer and Autumn/Winter.

At this point a question may come to mind — if identification is so easy, why is it that people manage to poison themselves, even when they have been picking and eating wild mushrooms for years? There are several answers to this. The first is that habit breeds carelessness. If you have been picking mushrooms in the same spot for years, it is likely that you will not look closely at

16

each specimen and even that you will allow young children to help you, in which case there is always a possibility (particularly when gathering 'field' mushrooms) that an *Amanita phalloïdes* may get into your basket unobserved, due to superficial similarities between the two. In theory this should never happen as *Amanita phalloïdes* grows in woods and not fields, but one must bear in mind that most fields were woods at one time and the possibility therefore exists of finding one springing up amongst 'field' mushrooms. Secondly, very young and unopened specimens of different mushrooms can look very similar, and it is therefore imperative to gather only those that have developed sufficiently for their characteristics to have become obvious. Thirdly, like any fruit or vegetable, you should eat only those that are in their prime; you should no more eat a rotting mushroom than a rotting tomato. Fourthly, *all* mushrooms, including 'shop' mushrooms, are fairly heavy to digest and therefore a surfeit of them can cause, in some people, digestive problems which are all too easily exacerbated by the fear of having eaten something poisonous. An acquaintance of mine made himself ill by this method; an analysis of the 'field' mushrooms he had eaten showed that they were not poisonous, but he had managed to eat several pounds of them for breakfast! As a result of this he has — unsurprisingly — become allergic to them, but there are also some people who are naturally allergic to them. Fifthly, mistrust of what one is eating is sufficient in itself to bring on nausea; British friends of mine have felt unwell after eating *cèpes* because, as one of them put it: "I felt suspicious of those toadstools as soon as they were put on the table!" Sixthly, it is possible to get over-enthusiastic and to decide to try fungi which *are not listed as poisonous. DO NOT DO THIS.*

This book shows those fungi that are known to be poisonous and those that are known to be not only edible but delicious. Apart from these, there are literally thousands of others which are not worth eating, or taste awful, or which could possibly do you various kinds of minor harm — therefore, leave them well alone.

When asked to identify such fungi, I am almost invariably asked: "Can I eat these or are they poisonous?" I have to answer that they may do harm but that in any case they are not worth eating; the question should be: "I think these are edible mushrooms but could you check them to make sure?" In other words, think positively; gather only those mushrooms which you are sure are the edible ones shown in this book, and in case of uncertainty ask an expert to check them for you. Do not think negatively that something that does not resemble a poisonous fungus must perforce be edible.

Do, on the other hand, banish from your mind those 'old wives' tales' which claim to enable you to identify poisonous fungi. Probably the most common of these is that you can eat a mushroom which has a ring. This must be not only the most common but also the worst error of all: the deadly poisonous *Amanita phalloïdes* has one. Another is that poisonous mushrooms change colour when cut or bruised; in fact this change of colour is common in edible mushrooms such as *Psalliota silvatica* (which stains red, whence its common name of the 'blusher', see Page 50), *Psalliota silvicola* (which stains yellow, see Page 50) — both of these widely consumed as 'field' mushrooms — and members of the *Boletus* family which turn from yellow to bright blue! On the other hand, the deadly poisonous *Amanita phalloïdes* does not change colour at all. Another common belief is that all mushrooms with pink gills are edible, the explanation for this particular one being almost certainly to help distinguish members of the 'field' mushroom family (whose gills turn pink and then black) from *Amanita phalloïdes* (whose gills always remain white). But whilst it is true that a mushroom with pink or black gills cannot be an *Amanita phalloïdes* it does not, of course, follow that it is therefore a 'field' mushroom. There are species which are suspect which also have pink gills, for example *Entoloma lividum* (see Page 38).

Other common but false beliefs are that a mushroom which has been nibbled by a slug is edible (slugs are very partial to all fungi, including *Amanita phalloïdes*), and that boiling in vinegary water will destroy any poison present (certainly not true of *Amanita phalloïdes*). There are other such strange beliefs, but the above will suffice to show that none of them should be believed in.

Having got all that out of the way, let us now return to a more detailed study of our three main groups of fungi. I have already said that the one which contains deadly poisonous fungi is the one that has gills; let me repeat again that one should never eat a mushroom with gills unless it has been identified with certainty. This can only be done with certainty when its characteristics have had time to develop, so let me also repeat again that you should never eat very young and unopened specimens (or old ones either for that matter, but it is unlikely that you would want to do so, as you are likely to find — except, curiously, in the case of *Cantharellus cibarius* and *Hydnum repandum* — that insect larvae are extremely fond of them once they are past their prime).

What then are the characteristics of the poisonous members of this group? Detailed descriptions accompany each mushroom in the text of this book, but here is the place to set out the general guidelines which should ensure that one does not go wrong. The first is that practically all the dangerous members of this group belong to the *Amanita* family, and what all *Amanitas* have in common is that at their very young unopened stage of development they are totally enclosed in what looks like an egg, known as the universal veil, which they break through just like a chick bursting out of its shell. The chick, however, than walks away from the egg and no large pieces of eggshell remain stuck to it to provide visible proof that it belongs to the race of our feathered friends — such proof is, of course, entirely unnecessary! The *Amanita* can obviously *not* walk away from its egg, and the extremely helpful result of this is that the continued presence of this egg, or veil, even at the adult stage, can enable us to identify with certainty the members of this family.

What does it look like? There are three types, although the third is really extremely similar to the second. The first consists of a solid membraneous 'egg' which is torn by the mushroom as it grows through it and which remains at the base of the stalk in the form of a bag: no traces of it remain attached to the cap of the mushroom. This is called the volva (see fig. 1, p. 16). To this type belong the deadly poisonous *Amanita phalloïdes, Amanita virosa* and *Amanita verna.*

The second type consists of an egg which has a very soft top. This remains attached to the cap as the mushroom bursts through and which is evidenced by the presence of a number of small patches or flecks. The bottom part of the egg, or volva, remains attached to the base of the stalk in the form of thickish whirls or ridges (see fig. 2, p. 16). To this type belong the dangerous *Amanita pantherina* and *Amanita muscaria* (see Pages 34 & 31). The third type differs from the second only in that the volva, being extremely fragile, disappears completely, otherwise the cap carries the same patches or flecks (see fig. 3, p. 16). To this type belongs *Amanita spissa,* which some mycologists consider edible but which is best left well alone, due to its close similarity to *Amanita pantherina.*

As this family is responsible for the vast majority of poisonings by mushrooms, we must make it a golden rule never to eat a mushroom which has a volva or patches of the universal veil on the cap, and if one is in any doubt whatsoever, to dig out the whole mushroom with a knife to ensure that there is no trace of a volva. There is, in fact, an absolutely delicious member of this family — *Amanita caesarea* — which, as its name indicates, was highly esteemed by the Caesars, but as it appears not to grow at all in Britain, and to avoid all possibility of confusion, it is not included in this book, although it is quite distinctive in that it has an orange cap and yellow gills and stalk.

Apart from volva or veil, the members of the *Amanita* family have two other characteristics in common. The first of these is that they all have white gills (with the exception of the above mentioned *Amanita caesarea*), and the second of which is that they all have a membraneous veil attached to the underside of the cap which falls away as the mushroom grows to form a ring around the stalk (the small *Amanita vaginata* is an exception to this rule — there always is one! — but as it is edible this has no importance). It is, therefore, imperative to remember when picking 'field' mushrooms that the presence of a ring does not prove edibility.

Other mushrooms with gills that are suspected of being harmful are small white members of the *Clitocybe* family (although some of its members are perfectly edible, e.g. *Clitocybe Geotropa*), small brown members of the *Pholiota, Lepiota* and *Cortinarius* families (particularly *Cortinarius orellanus* and *Cortinarius speciosissimus* which have been responsible for deaths — see Page 35), members of the *Inocybe* family, and *Entoloma lividum* (see Page 38). With the exception of *Entomola lividum* (whose attractive appearance may tempt some people to try it) *Cortinarius orellanus* and *Cortinarius speciosissimus* (which are now recognised to be deadly poisonous) these fungi are not included in this book for the simple reason that, unlike the poisonous members of the *Amanita* family, they bear no resemblance to the edible varieties described and can only represent a danger for the foolhardy.

Let us now examine our second group of mushrooms, those which have tubes or look like a sponge underneath their caps. To this group belongs *Boletus edulis* (*cèpe* or 'penny bun', see Page 66), considered by many connoisseurs to be the finest mushroom of all, avidly searched for by mushroom eaters all over Europe, and yet curiously neglected in Britain. This really is surprising since it cannot be confused with anything toxic or dangerous at all. The only member of the *Boletus* family which has ever been viewed with any suspicion at all (and even then probably unjustly, according to many experts) is *Boletus satanas* (see Page 39) which can be distinguished quite clearly by its white-greyish cap, red tubes or 'sponge' and red-veined stalk. There are other members of this family which have a bitter taste (*Boletus variegatus, Boletus calopus*) and others which are not worth eating, but none of them can do you any harm. In view of this, the beginner is well advised to make the *cèpe* the quarry of his first forays into the woods.

The third group of mushrooms, those which have little spikes underneath their caps, is only mentioned because there are no poisonous members of this group, and because it includes one variety which is very common and is widely eaten in some parts of Europe, and has in common with *Cantherellus cibarius* (the *girolle* or *chanterelle*, see Page 58) that it is almost always insect and larvae free. This is *Hydnum repandum* (see Page 87) which, together with the *cèpe* and the *girolle*, must be the easiest mushroom to recognise of all; it is known in France as 'le pied de mouton'.

Finally, a brief word about 'habitat'. A section is devoted to this for each mushroom, but the following few general points should prove helpful.

First, whilst it is obviously true by definition that 'wood' mushrooms grow in woods and 'field' mushrooms in fields, it does not follow from this that you will find the former in the middle of dark, dank woods, and the latter in the middle of any field. 'Wood' mushrooms grow near to trees because they rely on them for their source of food, but nearly all of them also require a certain amount of warmth and light which are rarely obtainable in the middle of a thick and gloomy wood. Some mycologists suggest looking for *cèpes*, for example, in the middle of beech woods, but you are far more likely to find them on the edges of such woods, or in clearings, or on the top borders of drainage ditches or close to paths running through them. In short, look for places which are dampish but not wet, and which are open to the sunlight. 'Field' mushrooms grow in fields in which animals have grazed because their source of food is the well-manured soil which the animals provide; they rarely grow in fields where artificial fertilisers have been used.

Secondly, do not look for mushrooms in places which are covered with thick vegetation; in the battle for survival — source of food, light and warmth — it is nearly always the latter that wins. This has the advantage for the mushroom hunter that he will find most of his mushrooms growing where they are easily visible, that is where there is only leaf-mould, or shortish grass, or sparse vegetation such as fern.

Thirdly, whilst we have indicated the habitat which is normally most propitious for each mushroom, this does not mean necessarily that you will always find some in such an environment, or that they will *only* grow in such an environment. For example, the *girolle* will grow in different types of woods, deciduous and coniferous, and favours in particular mossy embankments and the borders of ditches, but there are many such places where they never grow, whereas there are others which do not correspond to their natural habitat at all where they can be found growing in profusion. I know of one such place which has been a hen-run for many years and yet where, in spite of the scratchings of the hens, and absolutely bone-dry soil, they manage to prosper in very large quantities. The survival instinct perhaps, inducing them to reproduce as fast as possible? Whatever the reason, many attempts have been made to try to understand why such mushrooms as the *cèpe* and the *girolle* grow in some places and not in others, in order to reproduce exactly the same conditions and therefore be able to grow them commercially; with the exception of some minor success with the truffle and *Pleurotus ostreatus* (see Page 94) all such attempts have failed dismally in spite of the immense financial rewards to be gained. Look primarily, therefore, for your mushrooms in the locations described under 'Habitat', but do not expect them to grow always and only there.

Fourthly, weather conditions are extremely important. As mentioned above, most mushrooms require damp and warmth, which is why Spring and Autumn are the best mushroom-hunting seasons. But, it follows from this that few of them will grow if the weather is continually cold and very wet, or if there is a lengthy drought. In the former case (the more likely in Britain!) it is advisable to look in places which are well-drained and receive as much sunlight as possible; in the latter, one should look in damp shady places such as on the banks of streams or ditches. It should also be remembered that they rarely grow continuously over a long period; when weather conditions are right they will spring out of the ground in a matter of hours, but when those conditions change their growth will immediately be arrested.

Fifthly, there is a wide-spread belief that the moon has a direct influence on mushroom growth. I have often heard it said that mushrooms only grow properly when the moon is full, that if they grow at all at other times they will be full of insect larvae. This smacks very much of another old wives' tale, but there is no doubt an element of truth in it in that the change of moon is often accompanied by a change in the weather. If this brings about heavy rainfall after a hot spell (or vice-versa) then the ideal warm, damp conditions, as described above, are created.

Finally, whilst most 'wood' mushrooms prefer the proximity of one particular type of tree, this preference may vary in one or two cases. The *cèpe*, for example, always grows under oak and horse-chestnut in the south-west of France, whereas in Britain it grows more readily under beech. The reason for this is no doubt that there is little beech in the south-west of France, but if the *cèpe* does in fact prefer beech, then why does it grow in such large numbers under oak in this part of France? As far as I am aware, the reason is unclear. Never mind; if you look in woods containing both types of trees you are likely to find not only *cèpes* but a number of the other edible species described in this book as well!

Happy hunting then, and may you fill many baskets full of delicious mushrooms, but *do* always use a basket; plastic bags, carriers and such like will crush your finds and make a mess of them. Do not be like a cousin of mine who was so superstitious that he believed that you would never find anything if you took any kind of basket or recipient with you. It happened often, as he prospected on his bike, that he would come across large quantities of *girolles* that — basketless — he had no means of bearing back home other than by stuffing them down his shirt and — belt and bicycle clips firmly in place — his trousers; you can imagine what state *girolles* and trousers were in on his triumphal return! This method is not to be recommended!

CHAPTER ONE

Recipes

Detailed recipes accompany each mushroom in this book, but some useful general points about the preparation, cooking and preserving of them can be made at this stage.

Preparation

Many people systematically wash all the fruit and vegetables that they buy, and this is a sound practice in that it ensures that all traces of insecticide that may remain on them are removed. It is highly unlikely, however, that any insecticide, fertiliser or other chemical product will have come into contact with your wild mushrooms and it is therefore generally not necessary to wash them, and even inadvisable, as this can reduce their flavour and savour. With some species washing is obligatory as their caps and stalks — particularly in the case of those that have holes or 'veins', such as the Morels (see Page 42) — can contain soil, sand, leaf-mould or even small insects. In the case of the large, clean mushrooms, such as the *cèpe* or the 'field' mushroom, it is normally sufficient to wipe them carefully with a damp cloth, and indeed most old recipes for the *cèpe* are adamant that they should never be washed — or, most heinous of crimes — plunged in boiling water before cooking.

Once your mushrooms are clean, do not proceed automatically to slice them as one tends to do with 'shop' mushrooms, unless you are in a hurry to eat them, as some wild mushrooms, such as *cèpe*, taste better if cooked whole, over low heat, for a lengthy period. The objection may spring to mind that slicing is necessary to make sure that the mushroom has not been invaded by insect larvae, but there are two other methods of dealing with this possible problem. The first is that as these larvae invariably begin by attacking the stalk, it is normally sufficient to separate it from the cap to see whether it has been attacked or not, and the second (in case of doubt) is to place the cap, gills or tubes upwards in a frying-pan over a low to medium heat; if larvae are present they will immediately wriggle to the surface where they can be easily removed. As previously mentioned, this is a problem which is practically never encountered with the *girolle* or 'pied de mouton' (*Hydnum repandum*); in spite of their gastronomic qualities, insect larvae just don't seem to like them!

Cooking

The next step is to find the best possible cooking utensil. Whilst undue importance should not be attached to this, it is clear that if the mushroom is to cook for a fairly lengthy time over a low heat, it must be in a recipient which will not burn it or make it stick. The various kinds of 'non-stick' frying-pans are therefore quite suitable, as are the old style cast-iron ones, and even glass-ware designed to withstand direct heat. The best kind of pan, however, is one made of thick earthenware: it gently diffuses the heat over the whole surface of the pan and yet keeps it in, which has the double advantage of allowing one to cook over the lowest possible heat and preventing the mushrooms from burning or sticking. Those who are lucky enough to have a kitchen range, such as an Aga or Rayburn, will find this ideal; an earthenware pan placed on a corner of it where the heat is low will cook your mushrooms to perfection.

Slow, gentle cooking is best for most mushrooms therefore, but some species contain so much water that this needs to be evaporated before the cooking process proper can begin — this is particularly true of the *girolle* (see Page 58), the 'blewit' (*Tricholoma nudum,* see Page 86), the *Catalan* (*Lactarius deliciosus,* see Page 74), and the *Charbonnier* (*Russula cyanoxantha,* see Page 63). The way to do this is to place them in a frying-pan, without oil or butter, over a high heat; the water will then run out of them and evaporate in the pan, or to be more precise will be reduced to a concentrated liquid whose flavour is re-absorbed by the mushrooms, thereby making them taste even better. Some people like to drain this liquid off and use it as a base for soups or for adding to other dishes, but in this case what is the soup's gain is the mushroom's loss, which is perhaps a pity. Whichever you decide to do, make sure that all liquid has evaporated before proceeding with your chosen recipe, or it will affect the consistency of the mushrooms — in other words it will make them soggy.

Preserving

As you are very likely to find more mushrooms during a successful outing than you are able to consume before they start to deteriorate, it is obviously sensible to be aware of a few simple methods of preserving them. The simplest of all is just to put them straight into your freezer, although this does cause some loss of flavour. Or you can prepare and cook them first before putting them in the freezer. Alternatively, you can preserve them in jars which are specially designed for the purpose — 'Kilner' jars are a popular make which can be found in many ironmongers' shops. The method is as follows:

(a) Prepare and cook your mushrooms according to the recipe you prefer.

(b) Put them in the preserving jars and place on top the special sealing disc provided which is held tightly in position by a screw-down ring.

(c) Place the jars in a pressure-cooker filled to a maximum two-thirds with water, and 'cook' for at least one hour. This will sterilize them and form a vacuum seal which enables you to keep them until you wish to eat them.

When preserving in this way, it is advisable to use oil rather than butter in the preparation, as re-heated butter does not have the flavour of fresh. Another method is to simply blanch the mushrooms for a few minutes in boiling water and then preserve as above, but this method has the one minor advantage of economising on cooking oil and the rather major disadvantage of destroying much of the mushrooms' taste.

Another well-tried and traditional way of keeping mushrooms is to dry them, and this can be done quite easily by running a needle and thread through them — but taking care that they do not touch each other — and hanging them up in a warm airing-cupboard. This is an almost foolproof method, however, only for young, sound specimens of small species which dry easily and quickly, such as *Marasmius oreades* (or 'fairy ring' mushroom, see Page 46). Large mushrooms containing a fair amount of water can start to rot before the drying process is complete.

There are other methods of keeping mushrooms for shorter periods of time involving the use of earthenware pots and covering with layers of goose fat or good quality oil, but as these are not readily available or cheap in Britain, and as these methods are at best short-term, we recommend that you use the previously described methods of preserving.

CHAPTER TWO

Poisonous Fungi

Identification and Habitat

Amanita phalloïdes
(p. 14)

Amanita virosa
(p. 30)

Amanita verna
(p. 30)

The most dangerous of all fungi, these three are fortunately easily identifiable. Typical of the *Amanita* family (see Introduction) they have a volva at the base of the stalk, a ring halfway up it, and white gills which do not turn pink or brown. The cap of the *Amanita phalloïdes* is normally light-green or yellow-green in colour but may also be white. *Amanita virosa* is almost exactly the same fungus except that it tends to stand a little taller and always has a white cap. *Amanita verna* is the almost exact replica of *Amanita virosa,* the only significant difference being that it grows in the Spring instead of the Summer and Autumn.

These three are the most common deadly poisonous fungi, so therefore keep in mind their characteristics: presence of volva, ring, white gills and green or white cap.

They normally prefer oak or beech woods which are not too dense, although *Amanita virosa* can also be found under pine, and *Amanita phalloïdes* in particular can grow in large numbers in favourable conditions. It is not totally impossible to find them growing in fields, however, because, as mentioned in the Introduction, most fields were woods at one time and may still contain in their soil the leaf-mould which the fungi feed off. Do not presume therefore that a mushroom growing in a field is automatically debarred from being a member of this highly dangerous family.

Amanita virosa and verna

Amanita muscaria

These fungi are so dangerous because symptoms do not begin to appear until the poison has been absorbed into the bloodstream and has attacked the liver and kidneys. Very often this can take several days, by which time it is too late to use a stomach pump. Dr. Bastien, a doctor from the Vosges in the east of France, has developed a treatment which is claimed to be successful in some 60% of cases — and which he has publicly demonstrated on himself on several occasions, after having deliberately eaten *Amanita phalloïdes*, in order to prove its effectiveness — but prevention is obviously better than cure, so therefore make quite sure that you do not eat anything which vaguely resembles these highly dangerous fungi.

Identification and Habitat

Amanita muscaria (p. 31)

This fungus must be the all-time favourite with illustrators of children's books! It's easy to understand why: with its bright red cap with white patches this is one of the most beautiful of mushrooms. Unfortunately, it is also one of the most toxic, although it is extremely unlikely to kill you. The poisons that it contains — muscarine and musrazone — make one light-headed and faint, and the latter in particular has an hallucinogenic effect which is similar to that of the drug L.S.D. Do not let this tempt you into trying them! Apart from the harm they may do you, you could also find yourself in trouble with the police, so leave well alone!

It is extremely common in Britain, particularly in late Summer and Autumn, and seems to prefer very clear and airy birch and oak woods, or grassy parks planted with oak and birch.

It is a typical *Amanita* of the second type in which the volva remains in the form of thickish whirls at the base of the stalk, and the rest of the universal veil remains attached to the cap in the form of white patches; it has a ring and white gills.

Identification and Habitat

Amanita pantherina (p. 34)

Fortunately quite rare, this fungus closely resembles *Amanita muscaria* and contains one of the same poisons: muscarine. It has a similar thick whirled base to the stalk and white patches on the cap and has the same white gills and ring; it differs from it only in that the cap is brown instead of red. There is an edible member of the *Amanita* family — *Amanita rubescens* — which is similar but reddish-orange in colour and which stains red when cut, but as it is not particularly delicious and can be confused with *Amanita pantherina,* it is not included in this book.

Amanita pantherina can be found in different kinds of woods, but favours oak and beech.

Identification and Habitat

Cortinarius orellanus (p. 35)

Cortinarius speciosissimus

It was not until the 1950's, when it was found to be responsible for a number of deaths in Poland, that this fungus (*Cortinarius orellanus* and *Cortinarius speciosissimus* are to all intents and purposes the same fungus) was added to the 'deadly poisonous' list. This may sound surprising in view of the fact that the poisonous qualities of such as *Amanita phalloïdes* have been known for centuries, but is perhaps not particularly so in view of the fact that it is more of a mountain mushroom than a low altitude one, is quite rare, and is so small and unprepossessing and unlike anything edible that few would be tempted to eat it. However, it has caused deaths in Scotland in recent years, so I have to repeat that you must only eat those edible mushrooms which are described in this book; to operate on the basis that if it doesn't resemble a poisonous mushroom it must consequently be edible, is to court disaster.

This fungus is extremely dangerous because it contains the Orellanin complex of toxics

Amanita pantherina

Cortinarius orellanus

which cause kidney failure, and (as for *Amanita phalloïdes*) the symptoms do not appear until it is too late for treatment — often up to ten days after it has been eaten.

It is a small fungus which has a coppery brown stalk, gills and cap. It has no volva and the ring is practically non-existent as, like all members of the *Cortinarius* family, it consists only of a few very fine threads which are nearly invisible. It can grow in both deciduous and coniferous woods, normally on high ground.

Identification and Habitat	There is no need to worry unduly about this fungus. It is included in the book because it is viewed with high suspicion in some regions of France, and is indeed capable of offending your digestive system, but it will not kill you.
Entoloma lividum (p. 30)	An attractive mushroom — and all the more reason therefore to beware of it — *Entoloma lividum* has a grey cap and pink gills; it has no volva and no ring. It prefers deciduous woods (particularly beech, oak and elm) and likes to grow near paths running through such woods. It has a Spring-time cousin — *Entoloma clypeatum* — which it closely resembles and which is edible, but this mushroom is not included in the book due to the possibility of confusion between the two.
Identification and Habitat	Like all members of the *Boletus* family, *Boletus satanas* has sponge like tubes underneath the cap instead of gills or spikes. Unlike *Boletus edulis* (the *cèpe*) these are red in colour. Its very bulbous stalk is covered with a red-veined network. Its cap is grey-white, and when bruised the flesh turns slightly blue. In a couple of these respects it resembles *Boletus erythropus,* which is not only edible but fairly delicious (see Page 70 for distinguishing features between the two).
Boletus satanas (p. 39)	*Boletus satanas* does not normally grow in

36

large numbers and is to be found in the same kind of location favoured by *Boletus edulis,* that is beech and oak woods.

It is generally agreed that this fungus does not deserve its evil reputation, that it is indigestible rather than poisonous. However, as there is no point in suffering from indigestion for a mushroom which has no culinary value, we have decided to include *Boletus satanas* in this section.

Entoloma lividum

Boletus satanas

CHAPTER THREE

Edible Spring-time Mushrooms

Many people believe that Autumn is the only time for picking mushrooms. Not only is this untrue, but there are, in fact, certain species which grow only in the Spring, and two of them are considered by many connoisseurs to be amongst the finest of all. First prize must go to the Morel (*Morchella vulgaris, Morchella rotunda* and *Morchella conica*).

Identification and Habitat

Morchella vulgaris
(Figure 1, p. 42)

Morchella rotunda
(Figure 2, p. 42)

Morchella conica
(Figure 3, p. 42)

These mushrooms are very similar in that they look like sponges stuck on the end of stalks! The difference between them is that *Morchella conica* is shaped, obviously enough, like a cone, is dark-grey or black in colour, smaller than its cousins, and is found mainly in hilly areas. *Morchella vulgaris* is lighter in colour, particularly when adult, larger and less conical, and is found at lower altitudes. *Morchella rotunda,* as the name again implies, is larger and more rotund than the others and its colour is light-beige.

There is another mushroom which closely resembles the Morels except that its 'sponge' is thicker and more convoluted: its name is *Gyromitra esculenta,* and although not such a delicacy as the Morel, it is highly esteemed in some regions. A word of warning however. *ALL* Morels must be well-cooked as they can cause accidents when eaten raw. This is particularly true of *Gyromitra esculenta,* and some experts even advise drying it as well before consumption.

Morchella vulgaris, rotunda and conica

Tricholoma georgii

Unfortunately, these mushrooms are not easy to find and do not appear to have one favourite habitat. Some mycologists claim that they prefer airy woodlands, others that they prefer parks and gardens, yet more that they like to grow where fires have been lit the previous year. My own experience is that they grow in short grass close to paths bordered by elm trees, but your best bet is simply to go walking in woodland and parkland from March to May or June, and see what you come across! Even if you don't find any Morels you will stand a good chance of coming across our next mushrooms: *Tricholoma georgii* and *Marasmius oreades*.

Recipes for *Morchella vulgaris, Morchella rotunda*
and *Morchella conica*

Morels in Cream

Ingredients:

1lb. (500 gms. approx.) morels

¼lb. (100 gms. approx.) butter

1 cup of stock

¼lb. (100 gms. approx.) cream

½ a lemon

1 large spoonful flour *or* 1 egg yolk

Wash the Morels carefully as their caps can contain sand and earth, then cut into slices. Fry gently until golden in the pan with half the butter, add salt, pepper, the stock and the lemon juice, and allow to simmer until the juice has been reduced by two-thirds. Beat together the rest of the butter, the cream and the flour *or* egg yolk, pour over the mushrooms and cook over a low heat for a few minutes. Garnish with chopped chervil or parsley and serve hot. Served on its own with croûtons, or on buttered toast, this dish is absolutely delicious.

Morels with Scrambled Egg

The Morel is the ideal accompaniment for scrambled egg.

Wash the Morels carefully, cut them into small cubes and fry them gently in butter until golden. Add salt, cover the pan, and cook gently for approximately three-quarters of an hour. When they are nearly ready, prepare scrambled egg in the normal way (but the consistency must be moist) and then mix the two together. Add a knob of butter and fresh ground black pepper to taste.

Veal Chops with Morels

The perfect partnership, it enhances the flavour of both! Prepare and cook the Morels as in the first recipe: Morels in Cream. Cook the chops in butter for a few minutes on either side, add salt and pepper, and then add the Morels to the pan. Cover and allow to cook over a low heat for a further five to seven minutes. A veal kidney (if you can obtain one) sliced and cooked with the chops will make this dish even more of a success.

N.B. The Morel can be very easily dried and loses none of its flavour in the process.

Identification and Habitat

Tricholoma georgii
(p. 43)

The English word 'mushroom' is a corruption of the French name for this mushroom, 'mousseron', and it is indeed quite likely that it was consumed more readily than any other until growers learnt how to produce commercially *Psalliota campestris* (in Paris in the eighteenth century), which is why the 'shop' mushroom is known in France as the 'champignon de Paris'.

Tricholoma georgii grows freely in Britain from April to June/July, and for this reason, plus its appearance, is very easy to identify. It looks very much like a 'shop' mushroom

45

Marasmius oreades

except that its cap, gills and stalk are completely white. It has no volva or ring or patches on the cap and cannot therefore be confused with members of the *Amanita* family. It smells rather strongly of flour. It can often be found growing in fairy-rings (although our next mushroom, *Marasmius oreades,* is more often responsible for these), but whether in rings or straight lines you will always find it growing in fairly large quantities. It grows mainly in parks and fields, on lawns and even in flower-beds, and whilst it seems to prefer the proximity of the odd deciduous tree (particularly elm) it does not grow in woods. Which is all the better for the mushroom hunter: cast a careful eye on your lawn before you mow it!

Identification and Habitat

Marasmius oreades (p. 46)

The fairy-ring mushroom par excellence, and whilst it is not as delicious as *Tricholoma georgii,* it is still worth eating, particularly as it is very easy to dry and can therefore be kept for use over the Winter when other mushrooms are in short supply.

Like *Tricholoma georgii,* it grows in large quantities in rings or straight lines, on lawns and in parks or fields and even flower-beds, but it does not normally like the close proximity of trees. It is a very common mushroom which grows in the Spring, Summer and Autumn, and even — in certain favoured places — in the Winter.

Although you are likely to find this mushroom in the same places, and at the same time of the year, as *Tricholoma georgii,* which is why it is called in French 'faux mousseron' (the false 'mousseron'), it looks very different. It is a smaller and more fragile mushroom which has a beige coloured cap and gills, and its stalk — of the same colour — can only be broken by twisting hard. It has no volva, ring or patches on the cap. The only mushrooms which have a similar appearance are *Mycena pura* (pinker in colour) and *Laccaria laccata* (smaller, with a browner, more shiny, cap), but as both of these are perfectly edible any confusion would have no unpleasant consequences.

Recipes for *Tricholoma georgii* and *Marasmius oreades*

Although rather dissimilar in appearance, these two mushrooms have in common a rather 'nutty' taste which makes the following recipes ideal for both of them.

Basic Recipe

After having carefully wiped (or washed if necessary) the mushrooms, fry them in a pan over a medium heat in butter with a little pepper, salt and lemon juice, then cover and leave to simmer over very low heat for approximately a quarter of an hour.

'Mousserons en Croûte'

Ingredients:

½lb. (225 gms. approx.) mushrooms

1 shallot

1 large knob of butter

1 lemon

Cut the mushrooms into two or three. Chop the shallot and toss it in the melted butter in the saucepan. Add the mushrooms, salt, pepper, and lemon juice. Cook for five minutes, add the flour and then the cream and the gruyère cut into cubes. Simmer gently for twenty minutes. Toast the slices of wholemeal bread and cover them with the cooked mushrooms. Eat immediately.

'Vol-au-vent' type frozen pastry cases, pre-

2oz. (50 gms. approx.) gruyère

2oz. (50 gms. approx.) fresh cream

1 large spoonful of flour

Salt, pepper

4 thick slices of wholemeal bread

heated in the oven, can be used instead of the toasted bread and will, indeed, add to the attractiveness of the dish.

'Mousseron' Soup

Ingredients:

1lb. (400/500 gms. approx.) 'mousserons'

4-6oz. (150 gms. approx.) fresh cream

2 egg yolks

$1\frac{3}{4}$ pints (1 litre) beef or chicken stock

1 lemon

Salt, pepper, nutmeg

Slice the mushrooms thinly and put them in the simmering stock. Add the lemon juice, salt, pepper, and grated nutmeg, cover and cook for approximately thirty minutes. Then put through the blender, pour back into the pan and allow to continue to cook very gently. Meanwhile, beat together the cream and the egg yolks and then add them to the soup. Reduce over a low heat for a further five to seven minutes.

N.B. The 'mousseron' is also excellent in omelettes; prepare in the normal way (see Basic Recipe) but substitute 'mousserons' for 'field' or 'shop' mushrooms.

Psalliota campestris, arvensis, silvatica and silvicola

CHAPTER FOUR

Edible Summer/Autumn Mushrooms

It is most certainly true that some mushrooms begin growing earlier than others, and for this reason it is possible to divide those that grow after the Spring into Summer mushrooms and Autumn/Winter mushrooms. However, I do not consider this distinction to be useful for the mushroom hunter because weather conditions can vary so much from one year to another that it is perfectly possible to find a late Summer mushroom such as *Psalliota campestris* growing in November, and an Autumn mushroom such as *Boletus edulis* growing in June or July, or even earlier. The following mushrooms are grouped in the order in which they are most likely to grow during the year, but do bear in mind that they can grow at other times as well. I have found *cèpes* in early July in the middle of a heat-wave when logically there was no possibility of their growing at all. Similarly, two elderly gentlemen who taught me much of what I know about *cèpes* and *girolles,* once showed me *cèpes* growing underneath snow at the end of December! One of these two was a retired professional soldier, and a member of the Free French Forces during the war. Such was his love of mushrooms that he told me that he always applied for leave at the end of September and beginning of October so as not to miss the best *cèpe*-gathering season! This man was in a class of his own. No mushroom could escape him, and to prove it to the rest of us he would not pick them but would leave a lighted cigarette on each one for us to find as we struggled along far behind him — it was his personal version of 'Kilroy was here!' I well remember having crawled on hands and knees some thirty yards along a muddy ditch overgrown with nettles, sloe, brambles and hawthorn, when to my great delight I came nose to nose with an enormous *cèpe*. On top of it was a lighted cigarette.

On a more serious note, a brief word should be said at this point about the truffle. It is not included in this book because the 'real' Périgord truffle (which fruits from November to February) is, to my knowledge, non-existent in Britain, and the 'summer' truffle (which fruits from June to October) extremely rare. Furthermore, you will need a trained dog or pig to snuffle it out for you, as it grows underground. However, if you look closely at the soil around, principally, oak trees and spot a small hole which is surrounded by an oily kind of circle which is attracting the attention of flies, and dig down, you just might be lucky enough to find one!

Your chances are considerably greater however of finding one of those varieties of 'field' mushroom which start to grow in the Summer and which are generally considered by most British mushroom gatherers to be the only edible ones: they are *Psalliota campestris, Psalliota arvensis, Psalliota silvicola* and *Psalliota silvatica.*

Identification and Habitat

Psalliota campestris
(p. 50)

To begin with, and most importantly, one should point out the differences with the deadly poisonous *Amanitas, phalloïdes* and *virosa.* All of them have a ring, but *Psalliota campestris* differs in that it has no volva and possesses pink gills which turn to brown and black with age, whereas the gills of the poisonous *Amanitas* always remain white. The gills of *Psalliota campestris* can appear white, however, when the mushroom is very young, and I must stress that this mushroom is not to be eaten until its characteristics have had time to develop.

As the most typical of 'field' mushrooms, its favourite habitat is fields in which horses graze, as well-manured soil provides its source of food, but just as you are consequently highly unlikely to find it in fields where animals never graze, so you are likely to find it in open grassy places such as commons or country parks where sheep, deer or other animals run free.

It is really the wild version of the 'shop' mushroom, and it can be extremely delicious, but like other mushrooms it is best eaten young when the gills are still pink, as the taste can become very strong and even bitter when it gets old and the gills turn black. Although this is in theory the only member of the *Psalliota* family, together with *Psalliota arvensis,* which is a true 'field' mushroom, you will in fact often find *Psalliota silvicola* (see Page 50) and *Psalliota silvatica* (see Page 50) growing in its company in open grasslands, although these latter two are supposed to prefer woods.

Identification and Habitat

Psalliota arvensis
(p. 50)

This mushroom is often confused with *Psalliota campestris,* and it is indeed very similar. It does tend to be larger, it always has a white cap without the slight feathering which *Psalliota campestris* often has, but it has the same pink gills which turn to brown and then black. It has no volva but has a double ring on its stalk whereas that of *Psalliota campestris* is single.

Otherwise, the same remarks apply; this is an excellent 'field' mushroom which should be eaten young.

Identification and Habitat

Psalliota silvatica
(p. 50)

This mushroom is also often confused with *Psalliota campestris,* as in spite of the woodlands association that its name suggests, it is often found growing in the same grassy places, although it does seem to prefer more shade and for this reason can often be found under gorse bushes which unfortunately provide it with natural barbed-wire defences.

It looks much like *Psalliota campestris,* having pink and then brown-black gills, a single ring on the stalk, reddish-brown feathering on the cap, and no volva. It differs in that its taste is altogether stronger and more concentrated than that of *Psalliota campestris*

53

(which makes it ideal for adding in small quantities to soups and stews) and in that it stains red when cut or bruised: it is for this reason that certain connoisseurs call it the 'blusher'.

The same remarks as for *Psalliota campestris* with the modification that this one really must be eaten as young as possible as its taste becomes overpowering with age.

Identification and Habitat

Psalliota silvicola (p. 50)

To my mind, this is the finest member of the *Psalliota* family. Like *Psalliota campestris,* it has a single ring, pink and then brown-black gills, and no volva. It differs from it in that it has no feathering on the cap, that it stains slightly yellow, and that it smells quite strongly of aniseed. There is another member of the *Psalliota* family — *Psalliota Xanthoderma* — which also stains yellow, but which is not dangerous and is easily identified by the fact that it smells of bleach and has a very unpleasant taste.

Like *Psalliota silvatica,* this mushroom is supposed to grow in woods, but it is also commonly found in grassland in proximity to other members of the *Psalliota* family.

Otherwise, the same remarks as for *Psalliota campestris* except that its taste is more delicate, even in rather aged specimens.

Recipes for *Psalliota campestris, Psalliota arvensis, Psalliota silvicola* and *Psalliota silvatica*

These four 'field' mushrooms can be used, like the 'shop' mushroom, in many different ways — in omelettes, soups, stews, as a vegetable with roast meats, etc. You will find that they are also delicious prepared in the following more unusual ways.

Raw 'Field' Mushroom Salad

Psalliota silvicola is particularly suited to this recipe

Ingredients:

1lb. (500 gms. approx.) or 6/10 'field' mushrooms (more or less according to taste)

1 fennel bulb

1 lemon

Olive oil to taste

Approx. ½lb. (250 gms. approx.) mussels (optional)

Salt and pepper

Peel the fennel and slice into thin strips. Wipe (or wash if necessary) the mushrooms and slice them also into thin strips. Place both in a salad-bowl, add the lemon juice, salt, black pepper and olive oil, and mix well. The mussels (not essential, but they do go well with this dish) should be placed in a frying-pan over a high heat until they open up, removed from their shells and mixed in with the salad. Serve cold.

'Field' Mushroom Salad, Sauce Vinaigrette

This is another, simpler, raw 'field' mushroom salad. Prepare a vinaigrette sauce by mixing together wine, vinegar, walnut oil and pine kernels (broken walnuts will do equally well). Wipe or wash the mushrooms, slice them into thin strips, pour the vinaigrette sauce over them and mix well. Eat immediately.

'Field' Mushroom 'Dip'

'Field' mushrooms make an excellent 'dip'. Simply cut into quarters and serve with a bowl of mayonnaise seasoned with lemon juice.

'Field' Mushroom and Celery Salad

Ingredients:

1lb. (500 gms. approx.) or 6/10 'field' mushrooms (according to taste)

8/10 celery stalks (according to taste)

1 shallot

1 large spoonful of strong mustard

A little tarragon

Wine vinegar

Olive oil

Salt and pepper

A slightly more complicated 'field' mushroom salad.

Wipe or wash the mushrooms and slice thinly. Cut the celery into small cubes, mix with the slices of mushroom, add pepper and salt. Prepare the vinaigrette sauce by mixing together in a bowl the mustard, chopped shallot and tarragon, wine vinegar and olive oil (3 parts oil to 1 part vinegar). Pour this over the mushrooms and celery and mix well. Serve with wholemeal or granary bread.

These salads can be varied by adding sliced avocado, crumbled egg yolk, shrimps, tinned tuna, peppers, etc. The addition of cold cooked macaroni or rice and a few spoonfuls of mayonnaise will also transform them into a more than acceptable supper-dish.

'Field' Mushrooms stewed in Red Wine

Ingredients:

1lb. approx. (500 gms.) or 6/10 'field' mushrooms

4oz. approx. (150 gms.) baby onions

This recipe is particularly suitable for more aged specimens and for the stronger tasting *Psalliota silvatica.*

Wipe or wash the mushrooms and slice them. Peel the onions, peel and chop the shallots, peel the carrots and cut them into cubes. Lightly fry the shallots in half of the butter in a saucepan over medium heat. Add the mushrooms and fry for a further few minutes. Add the carrots and the red wine, salt and pepper, cover the pan and allow to cook for fifteen minutes. Add the onions and cook for ten more minutes in the uncovered pan until the wine has evaporated. Add the beef

2 shallots ·	
3 carrots	
¼ litre approx. red wine	
2oz. approx. (75 gms.) butter	
1 cup beef stock	
Salt, pepper, bay-leaf	

stock and the rest of the butter, bring to the boil and cook for a few more minutes. Can be served on its own or with any red meat.

N.B. The 'field' mushroom fritter is as delicious as the 'Parasol' fritter. See Page 62 for the recipe.

Identification and Habitat

Cantharellus cibarius (p. 58)

This is the famous French *chanterelle* or *girolle,* avidly searched for and eaten all over Europe, and which is so distinctive that it can only be confused with its close cousin, *Cantharellus aurantiacus,* which is more orange in colour and considered by many connoisseurs to be even more delicious! There is no danger of poisoning yourself with this one therefore.

Even on your first mushroom foray you will have no difficulty in identifying *Cantharellus cibarius.* It is bright yellow in colour all over, is funnel-shaped, and the gills, which are, in fact, rather more like thin folds, run from underneath the cap to about halfway down the stalk. There is no poisonous or dangerous mushroom which looks anything like it, so if it's yellow and doesn't move — eat it!

One of the reasons why it is so popular is probably to do with the fact that it grows so freely. It can be found in both deciduous and coniferous woods, in ditches and on top of them, in cold damp places and hot dry ones, but it seems to have a preference for mossy embankments. It always grows in quite large numbers so that you will not find just one or two growing together, but anything from a

Cantharellus cibarius

Lepiota procera

dozen to a few hundred! You will also find that it is almost always insect and larvae free. With the *cèpe* and 'field' mushroom, this must be the most popular of all wild mushrooms.

Recipes for *Cantherellus cibarius*

Many connoisseurs consider that there is no better way to eat the *chanterelle* or *girolle* than in an omelette, but in our opinion it is even better as an accompaniment to white meats — chicken, rabbit and veal. Whichever way you decide to use it, it is important to bear in mind that it needs lengthy cooking over a low heat.

Chanterelles with Bacon

Wash the mushrooms if necessary — it often is! Cut thick slices of streaky bacon into cubes and fry gently in a pan. Add the mushrooms and cook over a high heat until all the water from them has evaporated. Add a very little salt and pepper and continue to cook over a very low heat for one hour. Garnish with chopped parsley and serve.

Chanterelles with Herbs

Wash the mushrooms if necessary, then cut larger specimens into two or four (leave small ones intact) and place in a pan with a little oil over a fairly high heat. After five minutes, drain off the water they will have exuded — with *chanterelles* this is necessary as they generally contain so much water that they will boil in it for too long before it evaporates. Place in a colander and leave to drain for approximately ten minutes, then reheat a little oil in the pan, return the *chanterelles* to it, add salt, pepper and chopped garlic and cook over a low heat for thirty minutes. At the last minute, add chopped parsley and serve with roast or fried chicken, rabbit or veal.

Alternatively, when mushrooms and meat are cooked, they can be mixed together in the same pan and left to cook for a further fifteen minutes.

Identification and Habitat	The common name — if not the mushroom itself — is quite well-known in Britain. This is the 'Parasol' mushroom, known as such for the obvious reason that it looks like one in its adult stage. It is a tall-standing mushroom (often up to a foot or more in height) which has a brown, feathered cap and stalk, and a ring, but which also has a thick swollen base to its stalk and white gills like members of the *Amanita* family.
Lepiota procera (p. 59)	

For this reason it is advisable to confirm your finds with an expert before consuming them, but once you have done so you will realise that you are in no danger of confusing this extremely handsome and distinctive mushroom with anything poisonous. There are dangerous members of the *Lepiota* family, but they are all very small, whereas the 'Parasol' is tall and does not really resemble them at all.

It prefers, in Britain, to grow in August and September, but (depending on climatic conditions) it can also grow in October and even November. It has a great preference for grassy commons and parks, and even golf-courses, and it also likes the proximity of gorse, although, unlike *Psalliota silvatica,* it will not grow underneath it. It can be found in fields but not commonly so.

Stuffed Parasol Mushrooms

Ingredients:

A few large parasols

1 large spoonful of groundnut or sunflower oil

4ozs. (100 gms. approx.) soft bread

1 large knob of butter

2 or 3 cloves of garlic

Parsley, salt and black pepper

Cut off the stalks of the mushrooms and throw them away as they are too fibrous to be worth eating. Carefully wipe the caps, or wash them if necessary, but only under gently running water as the gills are very fragile and are easily broken off. Pour a little oil on each cap and grill them lightly for a few minutes on each side. Knead together the bread, butter, salt, pepper and chopped parsley and garlic, and spread this stuffing evenly over the gills of the mushrooms. Replace under the grill and cook for a further few minutes.

Grilled Parasol Mushrooms

This is a simpler version of the first recipe. Prepare the parasols in the same way, then rub a little oil on to the top of the caps and place them under the grill with the gills facing downwards. Grill lightly for 2-3 minutes, then turn them over, place a knob of butter on each one, add salt and pepper and put them back under the grill for a further 3-4 minutes.

Parasol Fritters

Prepare the parasols as above, then cut them into four or six, according to size. Prepare the batter as follows: beat the eggs into the water and then add the sieved flour. Beat well to

Russula cyanoxantha

Coprinus comatus and the various members of the *Psalliota* family are also excellent prepared in this way

Ingredients:

2lbs. (1 kilo approx.) parasols

2 eggs

1 cup of cold water

2 cups of flour

achieve a smooth consistency. Heat the oil in the deep-fryer, dip the mushroom pieces into the dough, and then plunge into the hot oil. After about two minutes the fritters will be ready. Take them out, put them on kitchen-paper to absorb the excess oil, then arrange them on the serving-dish with sprigs of parsley and pieces of lemon. Delicious as a starter or to nibble with the aperitif.

Identification and Habitat

Russula cyanoxantha (p. 63)

This is the most common member of the *Russula* family. It is included in this book because, although not as delicious as the other mushrooms described, it is easily found and bears no resemblance to anything harmful. The only member of this family which is to be avoided is *Russula emetica,* which has a laxative effect; its bright red cap makes it easily identifiable.

The principal characteristic of the *Russula* family, and which makes them easy to identify, is that, unlike any other mushroom, they have thick white stalks which break in two exactly like a stick of chalk. They have white gills but no ring and no volva. *Russula cyanoxantha* has a cap which can vary in colour from dark-violet to grey and even pink, but it is most often violet, particularly when young. It has a close cousin, *Russula virescens,* which is not only edible but considered by many connoisseurs to be superior to it. As, however, it has a green cap just like *Amanita phalloïdes* I prefer not to include it in the book to avoid all possibility of confusion.

Russula cyanoxantha is extremely common, growing in almost every kind of wood, but most particularly near to beech, oak and pine, or a mixture of these. It grows freely over the Summer, particularly in August, but can also be found in large numbers in September, October and even November. You are well advised to eat only young specimens as they are swiftly attacked by insect larvae which, for some strange reason, far prefer this species to more delicious ones.

Recipe for *Russula cyanoxantha*

'Le plat du Charbonnier'

Ingredients:

1lb. (500 gms. approx.) 'charbonniers'

¾ to 1lb. (400 gms. approx.) smoked pork or bacon

1lb. (500 gms. approx.) small onions

bouquet garni

Large clove of garlic

2 shallots

Parsley

1 large glass of dry white wine

This traditional recipe from the Landes area of south-west France is named after the charcoal burners of this huge wooded region who presumably prepared this mushroom in this way; it is indeed still commonly known as 'le charbonnier'.

Cut the pork or bacon into large cubes and fry in a mixture of oil and lard over a medium heat for approximately ten minutes. Cover with cold water, add the white wine, bouquet garni, garlic and sliced shallots and cook gently for three-quarters of an hour. Peel the onions, cut the mushrooms into three or four and add both to the pan. Add salt and a little pepper and allow to cook for a further twenty minutes, covering the pan. If the sauce should still be too liquid after this time, remove the lid and boil until the sauce has been reduced. Sprinkle with finely chopped parsley and serve hot with wholemeal bread.

Boletus edulis and aereus

Boletus badius

Known in English as the 'cep' or 'penny bun' but perhaps more widely known under its French name of *cèpe,* this is not only one of the most delicious of all mushrooms but also one of the safest. The only other mushroom which closely resembles it — also members of the *Boletus* family — are delicious to eat as well, and there are no poisonous members of this family, as explained in the Introduction. Its delicious brothers and cousins are described in the following pages, but I have omitted one for the simple reason that it is really almost exactly the same mushroom (and indeed most people are incapable of distinguishing between them) which is a little paler in colour and grows in June and July, whilst *Boletus edulis* proper prefers September and October. For the record, mycologists call it *Boletus reticulatus,* but you may hear it referred to in France as the 'cèpe des fleurs', the reason for this being that it grows in early Summer when the flowers are in full bloom. All this is of interest value only, from a culinary point of view it tastes exactly the same as a *cèpe.*

Like all members of the *Boletus* family, *Boletus edulis* has tubes, which resemble a sponge, underneath the cap. These turn from white to yellow and finally green. The cap is brown, but of a lighter brown than its very close cousin, *Boletus aereus.* The stalk is thick and swollen at its lower end — this is particularly noticeable in young specimens, adult ones sometimes having caps of such enormous dimensions that the stalk can appear quite modest in comparison — and is covered at its top end with a network of fine white lines. It has no volva and no ring.

In Britain it grows principally under beech, but is also found under horse chestnut and oak. In fact it almost invariably grows under oak in other countries. As pointed out in the Introduction, you should look for it in places which are not too damp and which get a fair amount of sunlight and warmth. The top borders of drainage ditches in woods are amongst their favourite places.

Identification and Habitat *Boletus aereus* (p. 66)	Like *Boletus reticulatus,* this one is such a close relation to *Boletus edulis* that the differences are insignificant. It has the same tubes or 'sponge' which remain white and firm for longer than *Boletus edulis,* it has a dark chocolate coloured cap, and a thick white stalk which does not have a network of fine lines. Some people prefer this mushroom because of its firm texture, but it really tastes the same as *Boletus edulis* and is prepared in the same way. Some connoisseurs claim that it prefers to grow near horse chestnut trees, but you are more likely to find it under beech and oak.
Identification and Habitat *Boletus badius* (p. 67)	Together with *Boletus pinicola* (which is very similar except that it has a bulbous stalk) this is a close cousin of the *cèpe* which prefers to grow in pine woods, and is generally considered to be nearly as good to eat. The physical differences are that the stalk is fairly straight rather than bulbous and is light-brown in colour, the brown cap is much more slippery when wet, and the yellow tubes will turn slightly blue after a minute or so if pressed with finger or thumb.
Identification and Habitat *Boletus rufus* (p. 70)	I include this *Boletus* because, whilst not being as delicious as the ones described above, it is nonetheless nicer to eat than some other members of this family which are either bitter or tasteless (but innocuous) and because it is often found growing in the company of the

Boletus rufus and erythropus

Coprinus comatus

cèpe; it is also often found growing near birch. Cooked with *cèpes* it has the further advantage of absorbing their flavour to such an extent as to become indistinguishable from them.

It differs from *Boletus edulis* in that, whilst having the same white tubes or 'sponge', it has a bright orange cap and its white stalk is covered with grey flecks.

Recipes for *Boletus edulis, Boletus aereus, Boletus badius* and *Boletus rufus*

Cèpes à la Bordelaise

This is the traditional recipe of the south-west of France. Wipe the *cèpes* clean with a damp cloth, they should never be washed. Separate the stalks from the caps, finely peel the stalks and slice them thickly, then put them to one side. Take a thick-bottomed non-stick or earthenware pan of the kind already described and place over a medium heat. Add enough groundnut or sunflower oil to generously cover the bottom of the pan (in the Landes region goose-fat is often used instead) and then place the caps, tubes uppermost, in it and cook just long enough — a couple of minutes is sufficient — for any water or insect larvae they may contain to rise to the surface. Remove them from the pan, place them, tubes downwards, on a dry cloth or kitchen paper and wipe them carefully. Now place the sliced stalks in the pan and cook quickly on both sides — five minutes is sufficient. Remove the stalks, throw away the used cooking oil, and pour a generous amount of fresh oil into the pan. Replace the sliced stalks, put the caps, tubes downwards, on top of them, add salt and pepper and cook for half-an-hour over a medium heat. The object of this is to evaporate any water that may be left in the mushrooms. After this, cook over a very low heat for one and a half to two hours (or for up to two days on the corner of a cooking range, according to some country people!). The final step is to chop together garlic and parsley, scatter this on top of the *cèpes* and cook for a further half-hour before placing in the serving-dish.

Cooked in this way, *cèpes* are normally served with roast beef, veal or chicken, or with 'confit d'oie' (potted goose). As the latter is hard to find in Britain you can substitute for it roast or fried pieces of duck. Otherwise, eat the *cèpes* on their own — they really are a meal in themselves.

N.B. Do not throw away the stalk peelings! Threaded together and dried in the airing-cupboard they can be used later for adding their special flavour to soups and stews.

Cèpes Sautés à la Sarladaise

If you have only found a few *cèpes,* you can make them go a lot further by mixing them with sautéd potatoes.

Cut the *cèpes* into pieces and fry them gently for approximately half-an-hour. Cut the potatoes into small squares and sauté them in another pan. When both are cooked, mix them together and add chopped garlic and parsley. Some people who know this recipe call it 'pommes de terre Sarladaise', but the real dish which bears this name is a mixture of potatoes and truffles.

Fried Cèpe Cubes

Here's a quick, convenient and novel way of cooking *cèpes* when you haven't the time for one of the preceeding recipes. Cut the caps and stalks into small squares and . . . simply deep-fry them! Add garlic and parsley and you will see that these are 'chips' with a difference!

Lactarius deliciosus

Craterellus cornucopiodes

Gros Cèpes à la Landaise

This is an old recipe from the Landes for preparing really large *cèpes*. Clean the *cèpes* as already indicated, and separate the cap from the stalk. For this recipe only the cap is used, but with *cèpes* of this size you will probably discover that the stalk has become too fibrous to be used in any case. Dot the cap all over with small pieces of garlic, place in a pan, tubes downwards, add plenty of oil, salt and pepper, and cook in the oven for approximately one hour.

Ragoût of Cèpes

Ingredients:

A dozen *cèpes*

3 slices of parma ham, or unsmoked bacon

1 or 2 onions or 3 shallots

1 glass of white wine

1 small glass of madeira

1 smallish bunch of white grapes

1 bouquet garni

1 spoonful of fat (preferably goose)

Salt and pepper

Chop the ham or bacon and fry it in the melted fat with the onion. Cut the stalks and the caps of the *cèpes* into large pieces, add to the pan and fry for a further few minutes. Add the white wine and the bouquet garni and cook for half-an-hour over a medium heat. The peeled and pipped grapes, the madeira and the salt and pepper should then be added, and the ragoût simmered for a further twenty minutes.

To each his taste, and some people hold this *Boletus* in high esteem, though in my opinion its flavour is rather insignificant. It has the advantage, however, of growing in large numbers in Britain, and you are very likely to come across it when looking for *cèpes,* that is, in beech and oak woods, but also in parks where these trees grow.

It is very distinctive in that its stalk is covered with an enormous number of tiny red dots, its tubes or 'sponge' are bright red, and if you break off a piece you will see its yellow flesh instantly turn to a bright blue. The differences with *Boletus satanas* (see Page 39) are that *Boletus erythropus* has a brown cap instead of a grey-white one, its flesh is yellow instead of white, and it turns a more startling blue in both speed and shade! Do not let this put you off, it does not mean that the mushroom is poisonous, on the contrary, it enables you to identify it as being edible. It has a close relation in *Boletus luridus,* which looks exactly the same (and is equally edible) except that its stalk is covered with a network of red lines instead of dots.

Recipes for *Boletus erythropus*

**Boletus Slices
in
Breadcrumbs**

As for the *cèpe,* avoid washing but wipe carefully with a damp cloth. Without removing the stalk, cut lengthways into thick slices. Beat two eggs in a bowl, dip the mushroom slices on both sides into the egg and then cover with fine breadcrumbs. Fry for ten minutes in hot groundnut or sunflower oil until crisp and golden and serve with a garnish of lemon slices.

Sauté of Pieds Rouges	Wipe the mushrooms carefully, remove the stalks and cut them into cubes, then slice the caps fairly thickly. Fry cubes and slices together in a mixture of oil and butter for three-quarters of an hour. Add salt and pepper, garnish with chopped garlic and parsley and cook over a medium heat for a further quarter of an hour.

Identification and Habitat *Coprinus comatus* (p. 71)	This one has the triple advantage of being extremely common, delicious to eat, and very easy to identify. Its long, white and cylindrical cap encloses the stalk like a sheath until it starts to disintegrate with age. The gills are white initially, but rapidly turn to black, which is why it is commonly called the 'Ink cap'. Its other common name, 'Lawyer's wig', comes from the shape of the cap and the feathery curls which cover its entire surface. It has a ring but no volva.

This is an extremely fragile mushroom, particularly when the gills have started to turn black, and should therefore be eaten as quickly as possible after gathering.

It can be found growing almost anywhere, but it particularly likes parks, lawns and grassy verges; I have even seen it growing on grassy roundabouts at the end of motorways.

It has a cousin, *Coprinus atramentarius,* which has the same white gills which turn to ink with age. This mushroom differs, however, in that the cap is much shorter, it opens out very quickly and its feathering is slight. It is not recommended for eating as it can cause flushing of the face and other unpleasant symptoms if consumed with alcoholic drink.

Recipes for *Coprinus comatus*

Like the 'parasol' (see Page 62) and the 'field' mushroom (see Page 54), the 'ink cap' can be prepared as a fritter filling, but it is best lightly cooked in butter or in a white sauce.

'Ink caps' in Butter

The stalk being fibrous, use only the cap. Wipe carefully (they rarely need washing), slice lengthways into two or three pieces and fry lightly in butter with a little salt and pepper for about ten minutes. Serve immediately on toast.

'Ink caps' in Cream

Prepare the mushrooms as in Recipe 1, but when they are cooked add a small pot of cream and allow to cook for a few more minutes. This is excellent with chicken and quality flatfish, such as sole and turbot.

'Ink caps' in White Sauce

Ingredients:

1½oz. (40 gms.) butter

1oz. (25 gms.) plain flour

½ pint (300 ml.) milk

Salt and freshly ground pepper

Prepare the mushrooms as in Recipe 1, then fry gently in butter for five minutes. Meanwhile, prepare a white sauce. Melt the butter in a saucepan over a low heat; gradually add the flour to make a roux (a smooth paste). Cook for one minute, then gradually stir in the milk. When all liquid has been added bring to the boil stirring continually. Lower the heat and simmer for two minutes and season with salt and pepper, then add to it the mushrooms. Put in an oven-pan, cover with grated gruyère, garnish with chopped parsley and bake in the oven for ten minutes. Serve with boiled ham.

Much appreciated in some regions of Europe and viewed as hardly worth bothering about in others, this mushroom has the advantage of growing in large numbers in its favourite spots, and of being seemingly indifferent to weather conditions: neither monsoon-like rain nor severe drought appear to affect it unduly.

Like all members of the *Lactarius* family it exudes a coloured liquid when the stalk is cut or the gills are rubbed. With other members of the family this liquid looks like milk, hence the name *Lactarius,* whereas in the case of *Lactarius deliciosus* it is bright orange in colour. This distinguishing feature is important as *Lactarius deliciosus* is really the only member of this family that you should eat, some of the others being capable of causing stomach upsets.

This mushroom has an orange stalk, orange gills and a cap which, initially pale orange, soon becomes partially or totally stained with green. It has no ring and no volva.

It is always found growing in sandy soil underneath conifers, particularly pine, which is why coniferous woods close to beaches are the best places to look. It grows freely in August, September and October.

You are well advised to only eat young specimens as this is another mushroom which insect larvae are extremely partial to, and older specimens are liable to be infested with them.

Recipes for *Lactarius deliciosus*

Simply fried or grilled, this mushroom tends to be rather dry and uninteresting but is greatly improved by preparation in one of the following ways.

Lactaires à la Méditerranéenne

Ingredients:

2-4lbs. (1-2 kilos) of *Lactarius deliciosus*

1-2 lemons

4-5 cloves of garlic

1 bay-leaf

1 or 2 pinches of thyme leaves

1 glass of dry white wine

6-8 large spoonfuls of olive oil

Salt and pepper

Carefully wipe, or wash if necessary, the mushrooms and cut them into slices. Heat the olive oil in a pan and when it starts to smoke add the mushrooms and the garlic, which should be well browned, before adding the white wine, the juice of the lemons, the thyme, the bay-leaf and the salt and pepper. Bring to the boil, partially cover the pan and reduce the liquid by approximately two-thirds. Eaten hot, they make a pleasant accompaniment for pork chops in particular, and eaten cold they go very well with cold meats as a kind of mushroom pickle.

'Pignasse Rouge' à la Catalane

Prepare the mushrooms as above, and fry them with garlic in the same way. Meanwhile, cut a piece of pork fillet into small cubes and fry until brown. In another pan, fry together finely chopped onion and skinned grated tomato until well-cooked, and then pass through a sieve. Put the pork, mushroom and tomato / onion purée together in the same pan and cook until tender.

Baked 'Pignasse Rouge'

This is a quick and simple recipe in which only the caps of the mushrooms are used.

Wipe carefully each cap, or wash if necessary, then chop finely together onion, garlic and parsley and place on the caps, gills facing upwards. Add salt and pepper, sprinkle with breadcrumbs and plenty of olive oil, and bake for twenty to twenty-five minutes in a medium oven.

This highly esteemed mushroom looks rather like the *girolle,* but it has a more pronounced funnel or trumpet shape (a common French name for it is 'Trompette de la mort'), no gills or folds, and its colour is light-grey to black. These distinctive features, plus its thoughtful tendency to grow in large groups in certain woods, make this one of the most desirable of mushrooms.

It prefers to grow in damp deciduous woods, particularly of beech and oak. You will need to look carefully however, as its colour and low profile can make it hard to spot, especially when growing on leaf-mould.

Recipes for *Craterellus cornucopioides*

This mushroom can be prepared in a number of different ways, for example, it can be cooked in the same way as the *chanterelle* or *girolle* (see Page 60), or stewed in white wine like the 'pied de mouton' (see Page 88), or in red wine like the 'field' mushroom (see Page 56).

However, in our view it is best prepared in the following way.

**Trompette de
la Mort in
Cream**

Ingredients:

1lb. (500 gms. approx.) mushrooms

½ lemon

2 large spoonfuls fresh cream

Chopped chervil

Wash the mushrooms (it is almost always necessary) and chop them, but not too thinly. Cook gently in butter with the juice of half a lemon, salt and pepper, for twenty minutes. Add the cream to the pan and allow to cook for five more minutes. Garnish with chopped chervil. Can be served on its own or as a filling for omelettes or with scrambled eggs.

CHAPTER FIVE

Autumn/Winter Mushrooms

As already pointed out for Summer/Autumn mushrooms, this label has no great importance because climatic conditions have as much to do with their growth as the seasons of the year. However, there are some mushrooms which have a definite tendency to grow at the end of Autumn and which prefer cold conditions. This makes them precious because not only are they amongst the most delicious varieties but they are to be found when other species are no longer available. Probably the most common of these is *Tricholoma nudum,* known in Britain as the 'Blewit', which in some regions of Europe — for example, the east of France — is considered to be amongst the finest of all.

Identification and Habitat

Tricholoma nudum
(p. 86)

This mushroom can be found growing from October until nearly the end of December. Its English name, 'Blewit', gives a clear clue to its identification, because it is indeed blue in colour. It common French name, hardly surprisingly, is 'pied bleu'.

It is easy to identify therefore. It has a blue-violet stalk and gills, and the cap is of the same colour in young specimens, but tends to turn light-brown with age. It has no ring and no volva. It can only be confused with members of the *Cortinarius* family which are also blue — particularly *Cortinarius albo-violaceus* — but apart from the fact that these latter have traces of a ring on the stalk and of a veil around the rim of the cap, there is no danger of poisoning oneself as they are perfectly edible although not particularly worth eating. The 'Blewit' has a light flowery perfume which makes it smell as appetising as it looks!

It is nearly always found in proximity to trees — deciduous rather than coniferous; it does not, however, grow in woods, but along paths or on compost heaps and particularly in light airy places where there is plenty of leaf-mould.

Identification and Habitat

Tricholoma saevum
(p. 86)

This mushroom is closely related to *Tricholoma nudum,* and it tastes very similar. It also looks similar, except that only the stalk is blue-violet in colour, and even then not always; the cap and gills are light-brown to russet. It has the same delicate flowery perfume as *Tricholoma nudum.*

It is generally claimed that it prefers to grow on lawns or in pastures and fields, but I have always found it in proximity to *Tricholoma nudum,* that is, by the sides of roads and paths and near to trees.

Recipes for *Tricholoma nudum* and *Tricholoma saevum*

'Pieds Bleus' à la Lorraine

This is a traditional recipe from the east of France, and — to our mind — much the best way of preparing these fragrant mushrooms.

Wipe the 'blewits' carefully (or wash if necessary). Cut large specimens into four and put into a pan with a large knob of butter over a medium heat. When all the water from the mushrooms has evaporated, turn the heat down low, cover the pan, and allow to cook gently for twenty minutes. Then add a generous measure of cream, salt, pepper, and a little grated nutmeg, and allow to cook gently for a further five minutes.

Baked 'Pieds Bleus'

Ingredients:

Approx. 20 'blewits'

¼ lb. (100 gms. approx.) smoked bacon

1 onion

2 or 3 cloves of garlic

4 slices of dry bread

Salt and pepper

Parsley

1 glass of milk

A little oil and butter

Grated gruyère

Paprika

Wipe the mushrooms (or wash if necessary). Detach the stalks and chop them together with the bacon, onion, garlic and parsley. Pour just enough milk onto the bread to make it soft, mash with a fork, and mix with the chopped stalks, bacon, onion, garlic and parsley. Fry this mixture gently for a few minutes in butter, adding the paprika (optional). Pour a little oil into a large oven-dish and place the 'blewits' in it, gills facing upwards. Put some of the stuffing on each mushroom, add a small knob of butter to each and bake in a medium oven for three-quarters of an hour. Finally, sprinkle with grated gruyère and replace in the oven or place under the grill until the cheese has melted.

Identification and Habitat

Hydnum repandum (p. 87)

This mushroom differs from the other edible species described in this book in that it has neither gills nor tubes under its cap, but small spikes. This makes it easy to identify and perfectly safe, since no poisonous or suspect fungus has this characteristic. From a distance it looks rather like a *girolle* with its creamy, almost yellow cap, and its tendency to look slightly funnel-shaped, which is due to denting

Tricholoma nudum and saevum

Hydnum repandum

in the cap and a downward curve around its rim. It is no doubt due to these dents giving it a cloven-hoof type of appearance that it is known in French as 'le pied de mouton'.

It is commonly found in October and early November, but it can also be found well into December. It prefers beech and oak woods, and tends to grow in circles very close to the trunks of the trees.

Whilst not being the most delicious of mushrooms, its frequency and late-season growth make it a most acceptable alternative when other species are no longer available.

Recipes for *Hydnum repandum*

'Pieds de Mouton' in Butter

As the consistency of the *pied de mouton* is rather dry, it is preferable to cook young specimens in butter, and to stew older ones in wine (see Recipe 2).

Wipe, or wash if necessary, the mushrooms; cut them into quarters and fry them in a pan, over a medium heat, in butter, for about ten minutes. Cover the pan, turn the heat to low, and cook for a further half-hour. A few minutes before the end of the cooking time, add salt and pepper and chopped parlsey.

'Pieds de Mouton' stewed in White Wine

A recipe tailor-made for the older *pied de mouton!* Quarter the mushrooms and fry them in oil for five minutes over a fairly high heat. Add to the pan a glass of dry white wine, salt, pepper, and a little chopped garlic, and leave to cook for a further thirty minutes in the uncovered pan in order to reduce and concentrate the sauce. Five minutes before the end of the cooking time, add two large spoonfuls of fresh cream and some chopped parsley, bring back to the boil and serve immediately.

Of all the mushrooms described in this book, this one is the least well-known and seems to be a particular favourite only in the sandy pine forests of the Atlantic coast of south-west France, where its common name is 'la pignasse jaune' (or 'le bidaou') as compared to 'la pignasse rouge' which designates *Lactarius deliciosus* (see Page 74), both names coming from the fact that these dissimilar mushrooms grow under pine trees.

Tricholoma equestre is easy to identify; apart from always growing under pine trees, in sandy soil, it has a yellow scaly cap, yellow gills and a yellow stalk. It has no ring and no volva.

The traditional method of preparing (and preserving) this mushroom is in vinegar, and it is eaten as a starter or to accompany drinks. Prepared in this way it really is very nice and deserves a better reputation, particularly as it can be gathered well into November and even December, when other mushrooms are no longer available.

Recipe for *Tricholoma equestre*

The best and really only way to enjoy this mushroom is by pickling it. Excellent as something to nibble with the aperitif or drinks.

**Pickled
'Bidaou' (or
'Pignasse
Jaune')**

Wash very carefully under running water as they are always full of sand. Use only the caps. Put them in a pan with salt, ten peppercorns, half a bay-leaf, a glass and a half of spirit vinegar. Cook over a low heat until the liquid has evaporated, stirring from time to time. Place in a screw-top jar with two shallots, one clove of garlic and one bay-leaf. Cover with oil and replace the screw-top.

Tricholoma equestre

Helvella crispa

| | This mushroom is a winter-time cousin of the Morel (see Page 42), growing mainly from October to December. Whilst not as delicious as the Morel, it is nonetheless excellent, having a nutty flavour which is peculiar to itself. |

Identification and Habitat

Helvella crispa (p. 91)

This mushroom is a winter-time cousin of the Morel (see Page 42), growing mainly from October to December. Whilst not as delicious as the Morel, it is nonetheless excellent, having a nutty flavour which is peculiar to itself.

It is absolutely distinctive, having a white cap which is twisted and convoluted like a rumpled piece of paper, and a stalk which is also twisted, veinous and full of holes. Like the Morel family it needs to be cooked as it contains the same toxins which are destroyed by cooking.

It prefers to grow along woodland paths, and more often in lines than in circles; it prefers deciduous trees, particularly beech, and is often found in groups of twenty or more specimens.

It has a close cousin, *Helvella lacunosa,* which has the same taste and looks exactly the same except that its cap and stalk are dark-grey to black in colour.

Recipes for *Helvella crispa* and *Helvella lacunosa*

Although not as delicious as the Morel, these mushrooms are rather similar in taste and can be prepared in the same way (see Page 44 for recipes). As their texture is rather 'chewy' they also benefit from lengthy cooking and can therefore be advantageously used in a chicken or rabbit casserole, to which they will add their delicate and distinctive flavour.

Identification and Habitat

Pleurotus ostreatus (p. 94)

To my mind, this is the only one of those species of mushrooms which grow on dead tree trunks or branches which is really worth eating. It has the two-fold advantage that it is quite delicious and can be found when all else has ceased to grow: I have even found them in January in extremely cold weather conditions. We can add to this that they are easily identifiable and grow in large clumps, so they are amongst the most worthwhile of mushrooms.

Their oyster-like shape (whence their common name of 'Oyster' mushroom), white gills and grey or blue-violet caps make them very easy to recognise. They grow on dead wood of all kinds, but are at their most prolific when the wood has become soft and lost much of its bark. They should be eaten young as they become tough with age.

Recipes for *Pleurotus ostreatus*

'Oyster' Mushrooms in Cider

Ingredients:

1lb. (500 gms. approx.) mush-rooms

1 onion

1 clove garlic

2oz. approx. (50 gms.) butter

4oz. approx. (100 gms.) smoked fatty bacon

³⁄₄ pint (½ litre approx.) dry cider

½ a dessert-spoon flour

½ a dessert-spoon butter

Salt and pepper

Chop the onion and the garlic, cut the bacon into small cubes. Wipe the mushrooms (they do not normally need washing) and slice them thickly. Melt the butter in a saucepan, add the bacon and onion and fry for two or three minutes. Add the salt and pepper, then the cider and chopped garlic. Bring to the boil, then lower the heat and cook for thirty minutes. When the mushrooms are cooked, work the flour and butter together until you have obtained a smooth paste. Add this to the sauce, mixing well. Serve hot. This dish goes very well with fried rabbit or pork.

Pleurotus ostreatus

Marinated Mushrooms

Ingredients:

1¼lbs. (600 gms. approx.) mush-rooms

10oz. (300 gms. approx.) baby onions

2 lemons

1 lime

1 clove garlic

4oz. (100 gms. approx.) grapes

2 sprigs of thyme

3 rosemary leaves

½ pint (¼ litre) water

1 glass dry white wine

Olive oil, salt, 1 large tablespoon of crushed black peppercorns

This recipe suits not only the 'oyster' mush-room, but also the 'pied de mouton' (*Hydnum nepandum*) and 'pignasse rouge' (*Lactarius deliciosus*).

Put a large spoonful of olive oil in a sauce-pan, add the mushrooms, cover the pan and cook over a low heat until their water has evaporated.

Put in a frying-pan a quarter litre water, the glass of white wine, the juice of the two lemons, four large spoonfuls of olive oil, pinch of salt, a tablespoon of crushed black peppercorns, the thyme, the rosemary, the clove of garlic cut in two, the grapes (which should have been left to soak for an hour in warm water) and the baby onions. Bring to the boil, then add the mush-rooms, cover the pan and cook over a high heat until the volume of the sauce has been reduced by three-quarters. Leave to cool and add the juice of the lime before serving.

This can be served as an 'hors d'oeuvre' or as an accompaniment to hot or cold meats.

INDEX